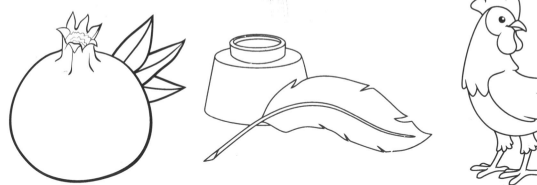

THIS BOOK BELONGS TO:

_____

_____

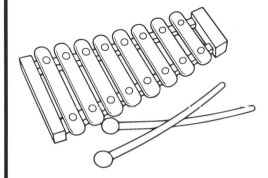

READY?
LET'S
BEGIN!

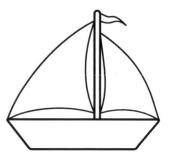

I SPY WITH MY LITTLE EYE, SOMETHING BEGINNING WITH...

A Is For

Apple

I SPY WITH MY LITTLE EYE, SOMETHING BEGINNING WITH...

B Is For

Basket

I SPY WITH MY LITTLE EYE, SOMETHING BEGINNING WITH...

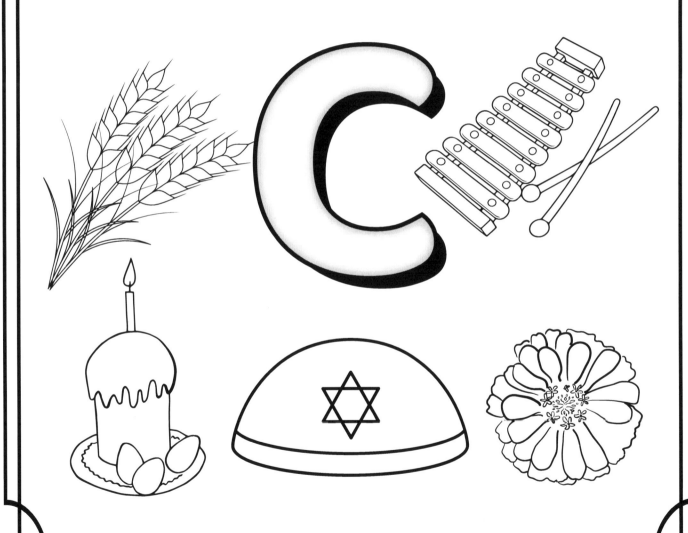

C Is For

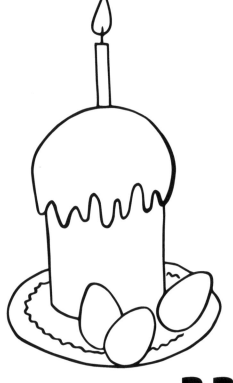

Candle

I SPY WITH MY LITTLE EYE, SOMETHING BEGINNING WITH...

D Is For

Dove

I SPY WITH MY LITTLE EYE, SOMETHING BEGINNING WITH...

E Is For

Egyptian

I SPY WITH MY LITTLE EYE, SOMETHING BEGINNING WITH...

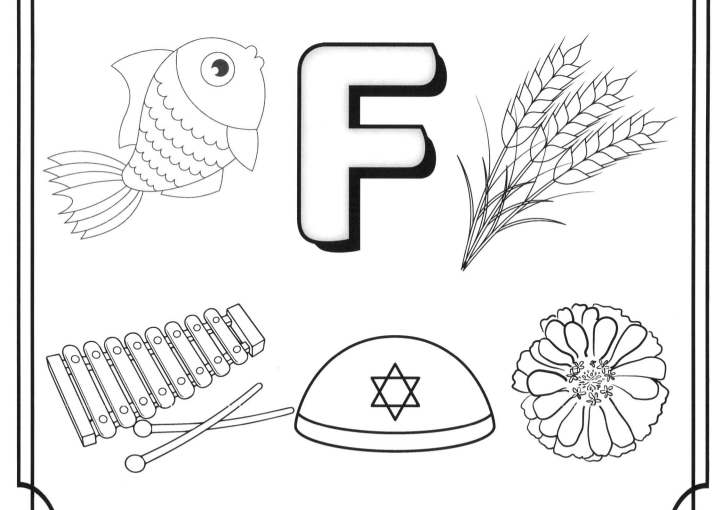

F Is For

Fish

I SPY WITH MY LITTLE EYE, SOMETHING BEGINNING WITH...

G Is For

Grape

I SPY WITH MY LITTLE EYE, SOMETHING BEGINNING WITH...

H Is For

Honey

I SPY WITH MY LITTLE EYE, SOMETHING BEGINNING WITH...

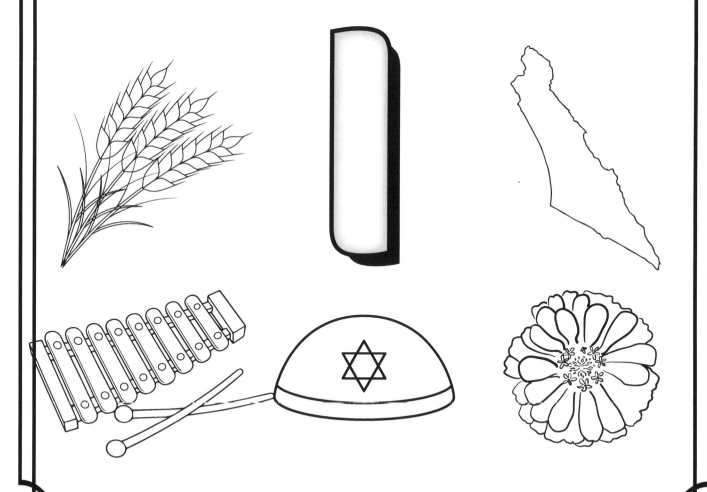

I Is For

Israel

I SPY WITH MY LITTLE EYE, SOMETHING BEGINNING WITH...

J Is For

Jug

I SPY WITH MY LITTLE EYE, SOMETHING BEGINNING WITH...

K Is For

King

I SPY WITH MY LITTLE EYE, SOMETHING BEGINNING WITH...

L Is For

Lamb

I SPY WITH MY LITTLE EYE, SOMETHING BEGINNING WITH...

M Is For

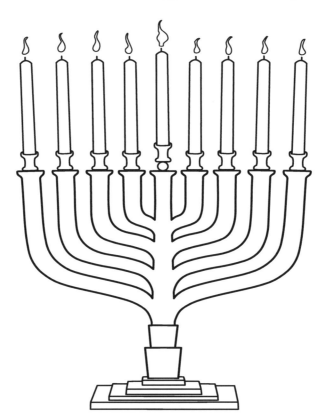

Menorah

I SPY WITH MY LITTLE EYE, SOMETHING BEGINNING WITH...

N Is For

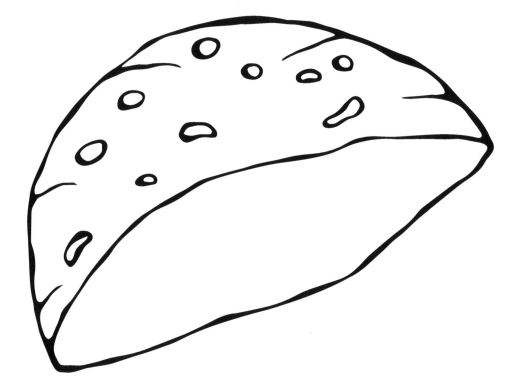

Nosh

I SPY WITH MY LITTLE EYE, SOMETHING BEGINNING WITH...

O Is For

Olive Oil

I SPY WITH MY LITTLE EYE, SOMETHING BEGINNING WITH...

P Is For

Pomegranate

I SPY WITH MY LITTLE EYE, SOMETHING BEGINNING WITH...

Q Is For

Quill

I SPY WITH MY LITTLE EYE, SOMETHING BEGINNING WITH...

R Is For

Rooster

I SPY WITH MY LITTLE EYE, SOMETHING BEGINNING WITH...

S Is For

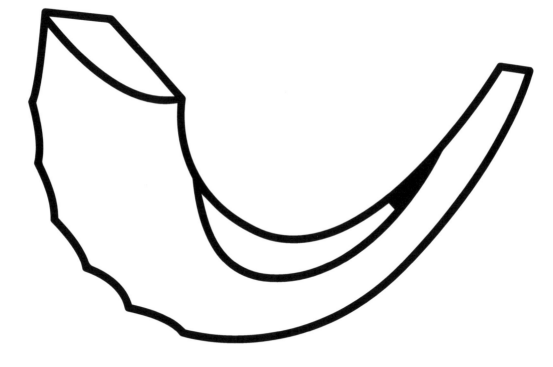

Shofar

I SPY WITH MY LITTLE EYE, SOMETHING BEGINNING WITH...

T Is For

Torah

I SPY WITH MY LITTLE EYE, SOMETHING BEGINNING WITH...

U Is For

Umbrella

I SPY WITH MY LITTLE EYE, SOMETHING BEGINNING WITH...

V Is For

Vegetable

I SPY WITH MY LITTLE EYE, SOMETHING BEGINNING WITH...

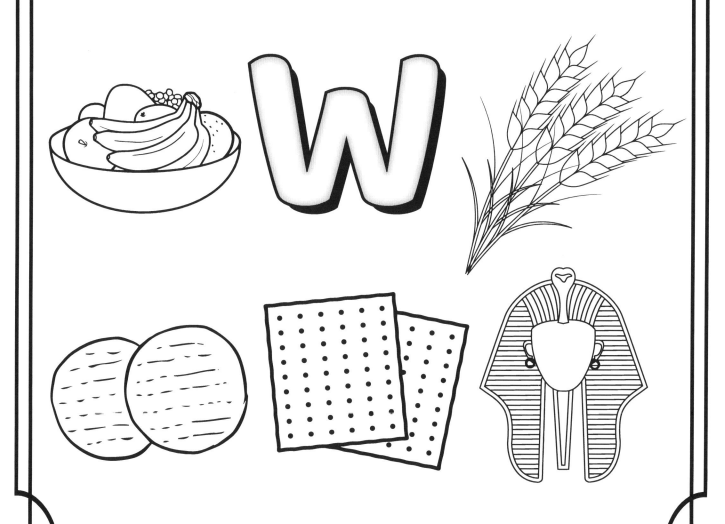

W Is For

Wheat

I SPY WITH MY LITTLE EYE, SOMETHING BEGINNING WITH...

X Is For

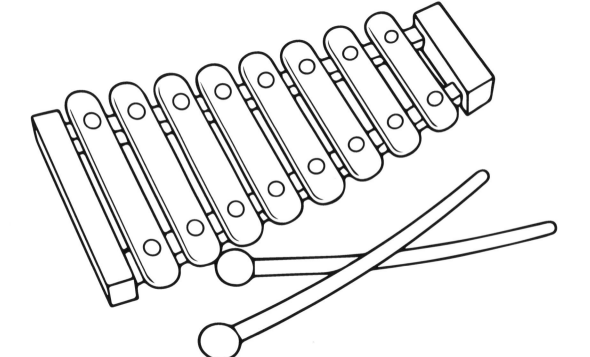

Xylophone

I SPY WITH MY LITTLE EYE, SOMETHING BEGINNING WITH...

Y Is For

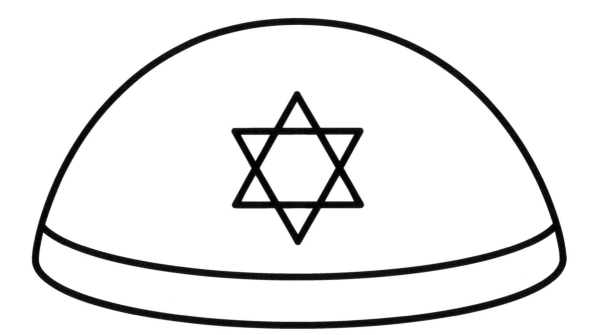

Yarmulke

I SPY WITH MY LITTLE EYE, SOMETHING BEGINNING WITH...

Z Is For

Zinnia

Made in the USA
Middletown, DE
17 September 2022